The Plant Cycle

by Nina Morgan

Illustrations by John Yates

HODDER
Wayland

an imprint of Hodder Children's Books

Titles in the series

The Human Cycle
The Food Cycle
The Plant Cycle
The Water Cycle

Words printed in **bold** can be found
in the glossary on page 30.

First published in Great Britain in 1993 by
Wayland (Publishers) Ltd

Reprinted in 2000 by Hodder Wayland,
an imprint of Hodder Children's Books

Hodder Children's Books, a division of Hodder Headline,
338 Euston Road, London NW1 3BH

British Library Cataloguing in Publication Data
Morgan, Nina
   Plant Cycle. – (Natural Cycles Series)
   I. Title II. Yates, John III. Series
   581.1

HARDBACK ISBN 0-7502-0692-6

PAPERBACK ISBN 0-7502-2127-5

© Hodder Wayland 1993

Series Editor: Kathryn Smith
Series Designers: Robert Wheeler and Loraine Hayes
Artwork: John Yates

Typeset by: DIS Fotoset Ltd, Brighton
Printed and bound in Italy by G. Canale & C.S.p.A.

Contents

A day in the life of a plant

Just like people, plants need food, water and air to live and grow. Although you cannot see plants getting bigger, they are always growing. Every day they are busy drinking in water through their roots, breathing in air and making food, in order to grow strong and healthy.

This clever picture shows how much this daffodil has grown in only one week.

Green plants need plenty of sunshine to make their food.

Most green plants make their own food inside their leaves. To understand how plants do this, think of making a recipe. To make a recipe we need **ingredients**. The ingredients a plant needs to make food are sunlight, water, good soil and air.

See for yourself

See for yourself how important sunlight is to plants. Plants move towards sunlight, because they need it to grow.

1. Put a small plant, such as a tomato plant, on a windowsill.
2. Watch what happens to the plant. By the end of the next day you will see how the plant has bent towards the light.
3. Turn the plant round so that it bends into the room. What happens during the next day?

How does a plant get ingredients to make food?

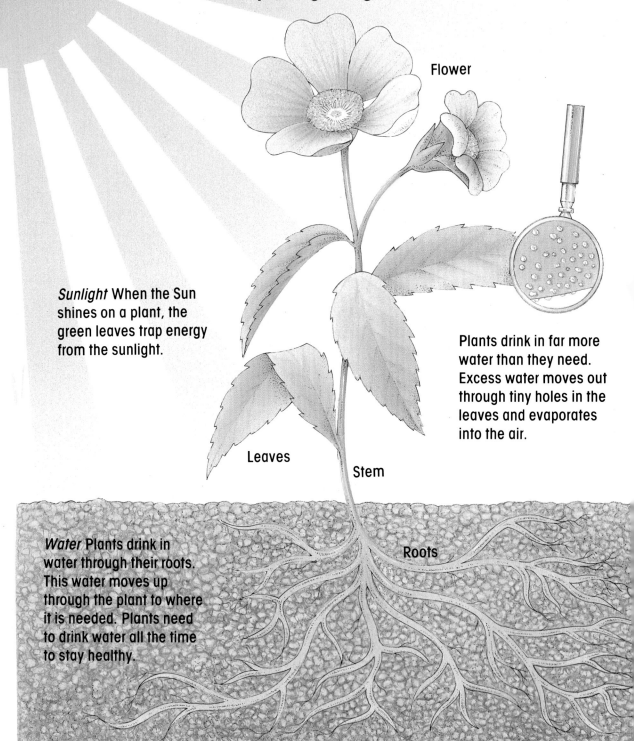

Flower

Sunlight When the Sun shines on a plant, the green leaves trap energy from the sunlight.

Plants drink in far more water than they need. Excess water moves out through tiny holes in the leaves and evaporates into the air.

Leaves

Stem

Water Plants drink in water through their roots. This water moves up through the plant to where it is needed. Plants need to drink water all the time to stay healthy.

Roots

Air We breathe in air through our nostrils. A plant takes in air through tiny holes in its leaves. The plant uses some parts of this air to make food. It breathes out the rest as waste.

If you put a bunch of flowers in a glass vase, you can see how much water they drink in. What happens to the water level after a few days?

Soil

Minerals Good soil contains minerals needed for healthy plants. These minerals dissolve in water. When a plant drinks in water through its roots, it sucks up some of these minerals at the same time.

See for yourself

Plants drink in far more water than they need. This water travels up through the plant, to where it is needed. When the water reaches the leaves, it moves out through tiny holes called pores, and evaporates into the air.

1. Water a small plant thoroughly.
2. Place a clear plastic bag over the plant in the evening.
3. Secure the bottom of the bag with an elastic band.
4. In the morning, what do you find on the inside of the plastic bag? Where did the water come from?

The reproduction cycle

How long do you think plants live? A few weeks? A few months? A few years? In fact, different plants live for different amounts of time. Some trees, such as the Giant Redwood, pictured here, live for many hundreds of years. Flowering garden plants often live for only a few months.

However long a single plant lives, a family of plants can live for much longer. This is because, like people, plants **reproduce**. Plants have found many special ways to make sure that they can do this. Sometimes only one plant is needed. Spider plants produce new plants from parts of their roots, shoots or leaves. Other plants, such as irises, can grow a whole new plant from just a tiny piece of root. The new plant will be exactly like the parent it grew from.

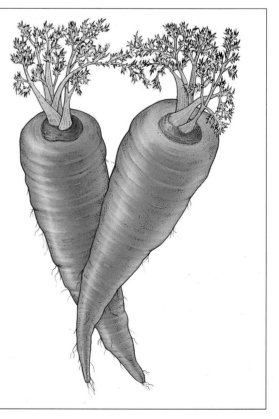

See for yourself

Some plants can reproduce from just a part of a root.
The carrots we eat are actually the roots of the carrot plant.

1. Cut off a piece of carrot near its top.
2. Place this in a saucer with a little bit of water.

After a few days do you see anything growing from the top?
What is the plant doing?

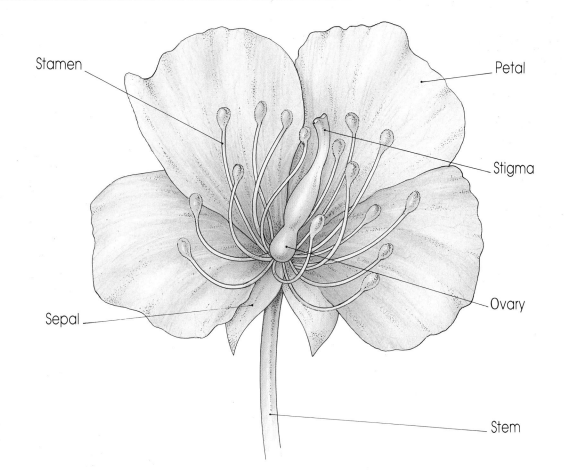

Stamen

Petal

Stigma

Ovary

Sepal

Stem

A typical flower head, showing the main reproductive organs of a flower.

Sometimes two plants are needed; a mother and a father. **Pollen** from the father plant joins together with **egg cells** from the mother plant, to make seeds. This is called **fertilization**.

Pollen and egg cells are found inside the flowers of a plant. Sometimes, if you carefully tap a flower over your palm, a fine dust will fall out. This is the pollen. The egg cells are found inside the **ovary**. You can see the ovary if you look at the picture on this page.

When the wind blows, the seeds in a dandelion clock are carried on the breeze.

So how do the pollen and the egg cells from two different plants meet? Usually the pollen has to find the egg cell. Some plants produce huge clouds of pollen which are blown around by the wind, until some pollen comes to rest on a mother plant. Others have brightly coloured flowers or sweet **nectar** to attract insects such as bees. Pollen sticks to the insects, who then carry it to other flowers.

Before a new plant can start to grow the seeds must leave the parent plant and land on good soil. Plants spread their seeds in many ways. Some seeds are blown about by the wind, some float on the water. Others are eaten by animals and left far from the parent plants, in the animals' droppings.

Some seeds are eaten by animals.

When the time is right, the seeds will grow into new plants. In time, new plants will grow and reproduce as their parents did.

... and finally the leaves.

... then the shoot ...

First the root ...

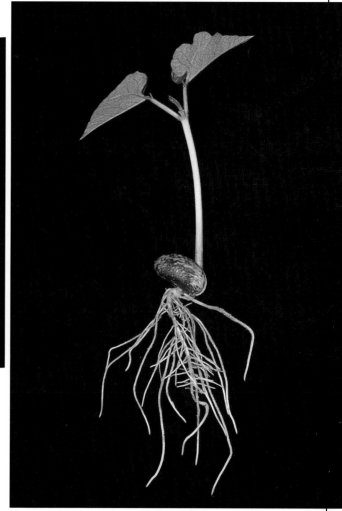

These pictures, from left to right, show what happens when a seed germinates.

Seasonal cycles

In spring many plants grow new shoots and leaves. New plants grow, too. Deciduous trees grow leaves again.

Through summer different plants flower and reproduce. Some make seeds from which new plants will grow.

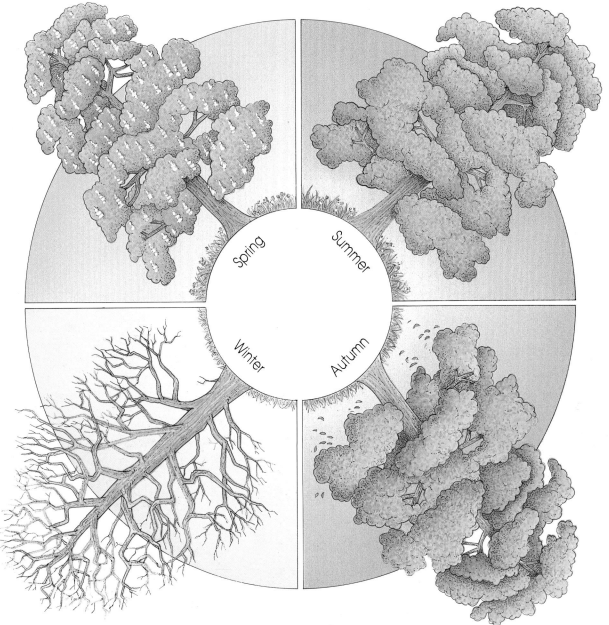

Spring

Summer

Winter

Autumn

In winter many plants stop growing and rest through the cold, dark, short days. Others die. Deciduous trees have no leaves.

In autumn many plants begin to die down or rest. The leaves on deciduous trees change colour and fall to the ground.

People do different things in different seasons. In winter we wear warm clothes, eat hot food and stay indoors when it is cold. In summer we wear cool clothing and play outside. Perhaps we even stay up later. Plants change with the seasons, too. The different weather tells plants when to rest, grow, reproduce and die.

In winter, when it is cold and dark, most plants rest. Instead of making new food, they live on food they made and kept earlier in the year, when there was more sunshine. Some plants die down every winter. They look like they have disappeared or are dead. In the spring they quickly begin to grow new shoots and leaves.

Winter brings cold, dark, short days, and perhaps snow. These changes affect all living things, including ourselves.

In winter temperatures drop and the earth freezes. Plants stop growing and some die.

Deciduous trees lose their leaves every winter, and grow new ones in the spring.

Evergreen trees lose their leaves all through the year, but because they are always growing new leaves they never look bare.

As we get near to spring the days begin to get longer, and the ground begins to warm up. There is more sunlight, so the plants come to life.

In spring the Sun's rays warm the soil again. This encourages plants to grow and trees to grow leaves and blossom.

When daylight lasts for the right number of hours a plant will flower. It will gently unfold its petals to the sunlight. These three pictures show a poppy flower unfolding its petals.

They begin to make more food. Many plants use the energy they get from this food to grow new shoots. Deciduous trees start to grow new leaves.

In summer the days become even longer and hotter. These changes make different plants act in different ways. Some plants will only flower and reproduce when daylight lasts for a certain number of hours. Others will reproduce before this. Each plant will flower at its own special time and leave behind seeds. These will grow into new plants the next year.

In the centre of this poppy you can see the stamens. They are covered with pollen. Pollen is needed to fertilize the egg cells.

When autumn approaches the days begin to grow cooler and shorter again. Deciduous trees begin to lose their leaves and other plants begin to rest. Some plants die.

In winter a lot of plants stop growing. They rest through the cold, short, dark winter days. They will continue their life cycle in spring, when the ground warms up, and the days get longer.

These changes which take place in spring, summer, autumn and winter are called seasonal cycles.

Life after death

What happens to a piece of fruit when you throw it away? It will probably begin to turn brown. It might become smelly and soft. Perhaps it will grow a furry covering, called mould. Finally it will shrivel up and disappear. In short, it will rot, or **decay**.

The furry covering on these strawberries is called mould. It rots the fruit.

This is what happens to plants too, when they die. Old pieces of fruit or dead plants may look completely lifeless. In fact they are seething with millions of tiny living creatures called **bacteria**. Although we cannot see them, bacteria are in the air all around us. They feed on dead plants and animals, and make them decay.

This fungus is growing on a dead tree stump. Like bacteria, fungus grows on dead material, making it rot. Eventually, this tree stump will rot away.

Have you ever seen toadstools or mushrooms in a wood? They grow on dead plants, trees and animals. They are **fungi**. Like bacteria, fungi feed and grow on dead **material**, and rot it.

When a plant or dead tree decays, it becomes smaller and eventually seems to disappear. This is because it is broken into tiny bits by the bacteria and fungi. These bits go back into the soil. The minerals the plant used when it was alive go back into the soil, too.

Dead leaves and wood eventually rot back in to the soil. The goodness they return to the soil is used by new shoots to help them grow.

Soon this goodness is taken up and used by new, growing plants. In this way, dead plants help new plants to grow strong and healthy.

See for yourself

The bacteria and fungi which rot plants work more quickly in warm places.

1. Cut a piece of fruit in two pieces.
2. Put one piece in the refrigerator, and leave the second piece in a warm place.

Which piece shows the first signs of the tiny threads of fungi or mould? Which piece decays faster?

Always changing

Plants, like people, are not all the same. On a tiny patch of ground there are usually many different types of plants. Each type has its own special needs. Some like sunny spots, others like shade. Some grow best in the shelter of other plants. Others like a certain type of soil. When lots of different plants live together like this, it is called a plant **community**.

These beautiful flowers are growing in a desert, where there is very little rain. Some other plants would find it very difficult to grow here.

Some plants find exactly what they need on a patch of land, and grow very well. They will grow strong and healthy and make lots of new plants. Other plants are not as lucky. They do not find everything they need to grow.

These four diagrams explain how succession works. The diagram below shows three plants which are growing on the same patch of ground; A, B and C.

Plant A finds the minerals it needs in the soil, it grows tall and strong, and becomes the strongest plant.

These plants can usually still grow, but they will be weaker and produce fewer new plants.

As the strong plants grow, they change the ground around them. Perhaps they are very tall plants and so make it shady. Perhaps they drink up a lot of water and make the ground dry. These changes can make the ground ideal for other plants, which, in turn, begin to grow well. Soon they become the strongest. This cycle of change is known as **succession**.

Succession also happens as the seasons change. Some plants grow best in winter, others in spring or summer. As the weather changes with the seasons, different plants become the strongest. Plant communities are always changing.

See for yourself

If you leave a patch of ground alone, many different plants will start to grow there. Leave one patch of lawn or playing field unmown during the summer. Does it have more types of plants than a mown patch? Do the same plants grow all summer?

As plant A grows tall, it makes the ground shady. Plant B likes shade. It grows strong and healthy in the shade of plant A and soon becomes the strongest plant.

Plant B needs a lot of water, so it makes the ground dry. Plant C likes dry ground. It grows well near plant B and in turn becomes the strongest plant.

Breaking the cycle

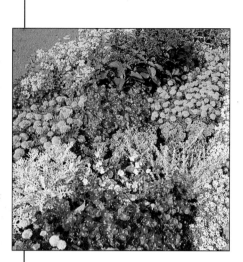

Gardeners spend a lot of time pulling up weeds, so that flowers can grow strong and healthy.

Some weeds, like this bindweed, can be very beautiful.

Whenever you dig up a patch of ground to make a garden, you are destroying a natural plant community. This is not always a bad thing to do, because gardens can be very beautiful and interesting, and bring much pleasure.

Many plants survive in our gardens because people work hard to make things right for them. For example, we pull out weeds to make it easier for garden plants to grow. The garden plants will not have to fight with the weeds for sunlight and **nutrients** in the soil. Weeds are not bad plants. They are just plants that are growing where we do not want them.

People also destroy plant communities when they grow food. If farmers want to grow wheat, for example, they have to make sure that the wheat plants have everything they need.

To start with, the farmer needs a field. He or she may have to plough up a meadow, or clear a forest where many different types of plants and animals live. If the farmer already has a field, he or she will have to get rid of many other plants in the field, which are weeds. Farmers may also want to add minerals to the soil to make it richer. **Insecticides** may be sprayed on the wheat to kill insects and to help the crops grow.

This farmer is ploughing a field. When a farmer gets a field ready to plant a crop, he or she has to get rid of any plants and weeds already growing there.

Many farmers set fire to rainforests. They want to clear the ground, so that they can use it for farming.

In Brazil some people have cleared huge areas in the **rainforests** to grow crops or to provide grazing land for animals. They argue that the wood from the trees can be sold to bring in money to the area, and that the land is needed to grow food.

Other people argue that the rainforests are too precious to destroy.

Over thousands of years, they have become the home to millions of different plants and animals. Many of them are not found anywhere else.

No one knows all the details of how the rainforests work, or what will happen if rainforest land is cleared. But it is clear that whenever we change the balance of nature it is important to consider carefully what might happen.

See for yourself

Crops grow best when they do not have to fight with other types of plants.

1. Clear two patches of ground.
2. In both patches plant several rows of radish seeds. Keep both plots well watered.
3. Carefully keep one patch free of weeds (be careful not to pull out radish plants by mistake).
4. Leave the other plot alone. Wait for three to four weeks.

Which patch grows the largest number of plant species? Which plot grows the best radishes? (If you want to do this experiment inside, plant your radish seeds in deep trays of soil. Add grass seed to one of the trays.)

Glossary

Bacteria   Very small living things which are all around us. They cannot be seen with our eyes. Some make living things decay.

Community   A group of plants and animals that live together in the same area and affect each other's lives.

Decay   When something rots.

Deciduous   Trees which lose their leaves in autumn.

Dissolve   To melt into something. Salt dissolves in water.

Egg cells   Tiny parts of a plant, found in the ovary. They are needed to make seeds.

Energy   Something needed to move, grow, breathe and live. We cannot live without energy.

Evaporates   Turn into water vapour (like steam from a kettle) or gas.

Evergreens   Trees which lose and grow leaves all year round. They never look bare.

Fertilization   The joining of male and female cells to form a seed.

Fungi   Plants which do not contain any chlorophyll (the stuff that makes many plants green). They live on rotting plants and animals.

Ingredients   Things that go into a mixture, to make a recipe.

Insecticides   Things used to protect plants from insects and diseases. Many of them are poisonous.

Materials   What something is made of.

Minerals   Substances found in the earth. Many

are needed by plants to grow strong and healthy.

Nectar   A sweet liquid found in some flowers.

Nutrients   All the things that a plant needs to remain healthy.

Ovary   The part of a plant where egg cells are kept.

Pollen   A powder in flowers which is needed to make new seeds.

Rainforests   Thick forests found near the Equator. These forests are full of many thousands of different plants and animals. Some of them have not even been discovered yet!

Reproduce   To produce young, or babies.

Succession   When new and different plants and animals move into an area, as conditions change.

Further reading

The Life of Plants by John Simmons (Simon and Schuster, 1990)
Plant Ecology by Jennifer Cochrane (Wayland, 1987)

For older readers
The Secret Life of Flowers by Bob Gibbons (Blandford, 1990)

Picture acknowledgements
The publishers would like to thank the following for allowing their photographs to be reproduced in this book: Bruce Coleman (cover picture, centre), 4 (J. Burton), 5 (Dr. E. Potts), 7 (E. Craddock), 12 (both, J. Burton), 13 (all, K. Taylor), 15 (bottom, J. Shaw), 16 (Dr. S. Nielsen), 17 (F. Prenzel), 21 (K. Taylor), 24 (top, M. P. Price, bottom, H. Reinhard); Geoscience Features 26 (bottom); Science Photo Library 18-19 (all C. Nuridsany & M. Perennou), 20 (Dr. J. Burgess), 28 (Dr. M. Read), Planet Earth 22 (H. C. Heap); Tony Stone Worldwide (cover picture, background), 15 (top, L. Adamski Peek), 27 (A. Sacks), Zefa 23, 26 (top).

Index